THE
Romantic
Rose

THE
Romantic
Rose

PHOTOGRAPHS BY

MURRAY ALCOSSER

WINGS BOOKS
New York • Avenel, New Jersey

To my father David Alcosser
who was a lover of roses

Copyright © 1990 Rizzoli International Publications, Inc.
Photographs © 1990 Murray Alcosser

This 1995 edition is published by Wings Books,
distributed by Random House Value Publishing, Inc.,
40 Engelhard Avenue, Avenel, New Jersey 07001,
by arrangement with Rizzoli International Publications, Inc.

Random House
New York • Toronto • London • Sydney • Auckland

Designed by Solveig Williams
Set in type by Rainsford Type

Printed and bound in China

Library of Congress Cataloging-in-Publication Data
Alcosser, Murray, 1935–1992.
The romantic rose / photographs by Murray Alcosser.
p.   cm.
Originally published: New York : Rizzoli, 1990.
ISBN 0–517–14702–5
1. Photography of plants. 2. Roses–Pictorial works. 3. Roses–Poetry.   I. Title.
TR726.R66A43 1995
779'.34–dc20   95-13263
CIP

8   7   6   5   4   3   2   1

Table of Contents

The Romantic Rose

The association of the rose with romance and mystery goes back far in time. In Medieval literature, we come upon this sweet-smelling flower already in fifteenth-century verse and many early poets likened their beloved ladies and mysterious muses to the fragrant rose. Shakespeare praises the rose especially for its perfume that endures after the flower is wilted because it can be distilled. He likens it to the very essence of the inner beauty of his lover.

In one of her gardening columns in the London *Observer,* Vita Sackville-West, chatelaine gardener of Sissinghurst in Kent, discusses the merits of scented roses. "It is an advantage for a rose to smell like a rose.... There are roses which are 'fast of their scent,' requiring to be held to the nose, and others which generously spread themselves upon the summer air.... 'Souvenir du Docteur Jamain' is an old hybrid perpetual which I am rather proud of having rescued from extinction.... deep red, not very large flowers, but so sweetly and sentimentally scented. Some writers would call it nostalgically scented, meaning everything that burying one's nose into the head of a rose meant in one's childhood, or in one's adolescence when one first discovered poetry, or the first time one fell in love."

Many of the old roses are now lost to us. The fact is that although some 20,000 varieties exist today, many have vanished forever. Among them are "Monstrous Four Seasons," "Belle sans Flatterie," "Black African," "Temple d'Apollon," and "Conque de Venus," all listed in the 1838 catalogue of the Durham Down Nursery near Bristol, England, when its owner, John Miller, went bankrupt at the very threshold of the prosperous reign of Queen Victoria.

On the other hand, new varieties are developed every year, to present ever larger roses, more thickly clustered petals, yet brighter colors, and newer, more distinct scents. Among such newcomers are "Dolly Parton," "Sheer Bliss," and "Sexy Rexy."

When new roses are bred and selected they are often named to honor celebrities, mark events, or to recall their color—"Grace de Monaco," "Peace," "Summer Snow"—or to emphasize their fragrance—"Perfume Delight." Among older roses there are some intriguing names that can only make one speculate. Who was "Albertine," "Nelly Moser," or "Honorine de Brabant?" Were they the dutiful daughters or respectable wives of rosarians who had endured and encouraged long years of experimentation or the unattainable objects of unrequited love?

The roses that flower wild in woods and hedges, untended and perhaps unobserved from summer to summer except by the bees that visit their caches of nectar and the birds who feast on their hips, provide the stock from which all cultivated roses stem. Their single flowers are mostly pale in color; white or blushing pink petals surrounding sparkling yellow centers. Among them, the apple scented rose or sweet briar is frequently smelt before it is seen. The dog rose that can grow into a 10-foot bush is the most common and provides strong rootstocks onto which more refined garden roses can be grafted.

Whether one favors a miniature bush with tiny, tight knots of blooms, a trained rose covering a whole wall, a standard rose trained as a tree, or a spreading hedge rose, one can find a wealth of varieties from which to choose. "I'm astonished," wrote Vita Sackville-West, "and even alarmed by the growth which certain roses will make in the course of a few years. There is one called 'Madame Plantier' which we planted at the foot of a worthless old apple tree, vaguely hoping that it might cover a few feet of the trunk. Now it is 15 feet high with a girth of 15 yards, tapering towards the top like the waist of a Victorian beauty and pouring down in a vast crinoline stitched all over with its white sweet-scented clusters of flowers."

For most of us the rose is a commodity bestowed by the florist. It is not a flower bought nor given as lightly as a bunch of tulips in the spring, chrysanthemums in the fall, or a potted cyclamen in winter. It is sought out for special occasions, be they milestones or mini-moments. There are occasions when no other flower but the rose will do. Fortunately we are no longer limited by season or latitude. Roses are flown in to delight our darkest winter days, to enhance festivities in the concrete jungles of our big cities and to elevate nice, small-town weddings into gala events.

Many are the memories we hold of moments when the rose played a decisive part, and in our thoughts there are always possibilities of future times when the rose may help to heal an injury, seal a union, or simply open doors and offer promise.

The Rose of May

Ah! there's the lily, marble pale,
The bonny broom, the cistus frail;
The rich sweet pea, the iris blue,
The larkspur with its peacock hue;
All these are fair, yet hold I will
That the Rose of May is fairer still.

'Tis grand 'neath palace walls to grow,
To blaze where lords and ladies go;
To hang o'er marble founts, and shine
In modern gardens, trim and fine;
But the Rose of May is only seen
Where the great of other days have been.

The house is mouldering stone by stone,
The garden-walks are overgrown;
The flowers are low, the weeds are high,
The fountain-stream is choked and dry,
The dial-stone with moss is green,
Where'er the Rose of May is seen.

The Rose of May its pride displayed
Along the old stone balustrade;
And ancient ladies, quaintly dight,
In its pink blossoms took delight;
And on the steps would make a stand
To scent its fragrance—fan in hand.

Long have been dead those ladies gay;
Their very heirs have passed away;
And their old portraits, prim and tall,
Are mouldering in the mouldering hall;
The terrace and the balustrade
Lie broken, weedy and decayed.

But blithe and tall the Rose of May
Shoots upward through the ruin gray;
With scented flower, and leaf pale green,
Such rose as it hath never been,
Left, like a noble deed, to grace
The memory of an ancient race.

Mary Howitt [1799–1888]

Pages 10–11: Brooklyn Botanic Garden,
Brooklyn, New York City

Right: The Walled Garden, Filoli,
Woodside, California

Left: Longwood Gardens, Kennett Square, Pennsylvania

15

18

O My Luve's Like a Red, Red, Rose

O my Luve's like a red, red rose
   That's newly sprung in June:
O my Luve's like the melodie
   That's sweetly play'd in tune.

As fair art thou, my bonnie lass,
   So deep in luve am I:
And I will luve thee still, my dear,
   Till a' the seas gang dry:

Till a' the seas gang dry, my dear,
   And the rocks melt wi' the sun;
I will luve thee still, my dear,
   While the sands o' life shall run.

And fare thee weel, my only Luve
   And fare thee weel awhile!
And I will come again, my Luve,
   Tho' it were ten thousand mile.

Robert Burns [1759–1796]

Pages 22–23: Old Westbury Gardens, Old Westbury, New York

Right: The Rose Garden in Woodland Park Zoological Gardens, Seattle, Washington

To —

Music, when soft voices die,
Vibrates in the memory—
Odours, when sweet violets sicken,
Live within the sense they quicken.

Rose leaves, when the rose is dead,
Are heaped for the beloved's bed;
And so thy thoughts, when thou art gone,
Love itself shall slumber on.

Percy Bysshe Shelley [1792–1822]

Pages 26–27: Old Westbury Gardens, Old Westbury, New York

Right: Longwood Gardens, Kennett Square, Pennsylvania

Field Path

The beans in blossom with their spots of jet
Smelt sweet as gardens wheresoever met;
The level meadow grass was in the swath;
The hedge briar rose hung right across the path,
White over with its flowers—the grass that lay
Bleaching beneath the twittering heat to hay
Smelt so deliciously, the puzzled bee
Went wondering where the honeyed sweets could be;
And passer-by along the level rows
Stooped down and whipt a bit beneath his nose.

John Clare [1793–1864]

37

Sonnet 54

Oh, how much more doth beauty beauteous seem
By that sweet ornament which truth doth give:
The rose looks fair, but fairer we it deem
For that sweet odor which doth in it live.
The canker blooms have full as deep a dye
As the perfumed tincture of the roses,
Hang on such thorns, and play as wantonly
When summer's breath their masked buds discloses;
But, for their virtue only is their show,
They live unwooed and unrespected fade,
Die to themselves. Sweet roses do not so:
Of their sweet deaths are sweetest odors made.
   And so of you, beauteous and lovely youth,
   When that shall fade, my verse distills your truth.
William Shakespeare [1564–1616]

Sonnet 18

Shall I compare thee to a summer's day?
Thou art more lovely and more temperate;
Rough winds do shake the darling buds of May;
And summer's lease hath all too short a date.
Sometime too hot the eye of heaven shines,
And often is his gold complexion dimmed;
And every fair from fair sometimes declines,
By chance, or Nature's changing course, untrimmed:
But thy eternal summer shall not fade,
Nor lose possession of that fair thou owest,
Nor shall Death brag thou wand'rest in his shade,
When in eternal lines to Time thou growest.
    So long as men can breathe or eyes can see,
    So long lives this, and this gives life to thee.
          William Shakespeare [1564–1616]

Right: Descanso Gardens, La Canada, California

Pages 52–53: Longwood Gardens, Kennett Square, Pennsylvania

Right: Brooklyn Botanic Garden, Brooklyn, New York City

Gather Ye Rose-buds

Gather ye rose-buds while ye may,
    Old Time is still a-flying:
And this same flower that smiles to-day,
To-morrow will be dying.

The glorious Lamp of Heaven, the Sun,
    The higher he's a-getting
The sooner will his race be run,
    And nearer he's to setting.

That age is best which is the first,
    When youth and blood are warmer:
But being spent, the worse, and worst
    Times, still succeed the former.

Then, be not coy, but use your time;
    And while ye may, go marry:
For having lost but once your prime,
    You may for ever tarry.

              Robert Herrick [1591–1674]

The Best

What's the best thing in the world?
June-rose, by May-dew impearl'd;
Sweet south-wind, that means no rain;
Truth, not cruel to a friend;
Pleasure, not in haste to end;
Beauty, not self-deck'd and curl'd
Till its pride is over-plain;
Light, that never makes you wink;
Memory, that gives no pain;
Love, when, *so*, you've loved again.
What's the best thing in the world?
—Something out of it, I think.
Elizabeth Barrett Browning [1806–1861]

Go, Lovely Rose

Go, lovely Rose,
Tell her, that wastes her time and me,
That now she knows,
When I resemble her to thee,
How sweet and fair she seems to be.

Tell her that's young
And shuns to have her graces spied,
That hadst thou sprung
In deserts, where no men abide,
Thou must have uncommended died.

Small is the worth
Of beauty from the light retired;
Bid her come forth,
Suffer herself to be desired,
And not blush so to be admired.

Then die! that she
The common fate of all things rare
May read in thee:
How small a part of time they share
That are so wondrous sweet and fair!

Edmund Waller [1606–1687]

From *Rubaiyát of Omar Khayyám of Naishápúr*

Awake! for Morning in the Bowl of Night
Has flung the Stone that puts the Stars to Flight:
　And Lo! the Hunter of the East has caught
The Sultan's Turret in a Noose of Light.

Irám indeed is gone with all its Rose,
And Jamshýd's Sev'n-ring'd Cup where no one knows;
　But still the Vine her ancient Ruby yields,
And still a Garden by the Water blows.

And David's Lips are lock't; but in divine
High-piping Pehleví, with 'Wine! Wine! Wine!
　'*Red* Wine!' – the Nightingale cries to the Rose
That yellow Cheek of hers to incarnadine.

And look – a thousand Blossoms with the Day
Woke – and a thousand scatter'd into Clay:
　And this first Summer Month that bring the Rose
Shall take Jamshýd and Kaikobád away.

Look to the Rose that blows about us – 'Lo,
'Laughing,' she says, 'into the World I blow:
　'At once the silken Tassel of my Purse
'Tear, and its Treasure on the Garden throw.'

While the Rose blows along the River Brink,
With old Khayyám the Ruby Vintage drink:
　And when the Angel with his darker Draught
Draws up to Thee – take that, and do not shrink.

Edward Fitzgerald [1809–1883]

Pages 76–77: The Rose Garden in
Woodland Park Zoological Gardens, Seattle
Washington

Right: Huntington Botanical Gardens, San
Marino, California

78

Left: The Cloisters, Fort Tryon Park, New York City

Pages 82–83: Brooklyn Botanic Garden, Brooklyn, New York City

81

Left: New York Botanical Gardens, The Bronx, New York City

85

Fall, Leaves, Fall

Fall, leaves, fall; die, flowers, away;
Lengthen night and shorten day;
Every leaf speaks bliss to me
Fluttering from the autumn tree.
I shall smile when wreaths of snow
Blossom where the rose should grow;
I shall sing when night's decay
Ushers in a drearier day.

Emily Brontë [1818–1848]

The Rose

A Rose, as fair as ever saw the North,
Grew in a little garden all alone;
A sweeter flower did Nature ne'er put forth,
Nor fairer garden yet was never known:
The maidens danced about it morn and noon,
And learned bards of it their ditties made;
The nimble fairies by the pale-faced moon
Watered the root and kissed her pretty shade.
But well-a-day!—the gardener careless grew;
The maids and fairies both were kept away,
And in a drought the caterpillars threw
Themselves upon the bud and every spray.
   God shield the stock! If heaven send no supplies,
   The fairest blossom of the garden dies.

William Browne [1591–1643]

June

June of the iris and the rose.
The rose not English as we fondly think.
     Anacreon and Bion sang the rose;
And Rhodes the isle whose very name means rose
     Struck roses on her coins . . .
The Young Crusaders found the Syrian rose
     Springing from Saracenic quoins,
     And China opened her shut gate
To let her roses through, and Persian shrines
     Of poetry and painting gave the rose.

Vita Sackville-West [1892–1962]

I Remember

I remember, I remember
The house where I was born,
The little window where the sun
Came peeping in at morn;
He never came a wink too soon
Nor brought too long a day;
But now, I often wish the night
Had borne my breath away.

I remember, I remember
The roses, red and white,
The violets, and the lily-cups –
Those flowers made of light!
The lilacs where the robin built,
And where my brother set
The laburnum on his birthday, –
The tree is living yet!

I remember, I remember
Where I was used to swing,
And thought the air must rush as fresh
To swallows on the wing;
My spirit flew in feathers then
That is so heavy now,
And summer pools could hardly cool
The fever on my brow.

I remember, I remember
The fir trees dark and high;
I used to think their slender tops
Were close against the sky:
It was a childish ignorance,
But now 'tis little joy
To know I'm farther off from Heaven
Than when I was a boy.

Thomas Hood [1799–1845]

Left: Old Westbury Gardens, Old Westbury, New York

Right: Butchart Gardens, Victoria, British Columbia, Canada

Pages 114–115: Longwood Gardens, Kennett Square, Pennsylvania

Spring Quiet

Gone were but the Winter,
   Come were but the Spring,
I would go to a covert
   Where the birds sing;

Where in the whitethorn
   Singeth a thrush,
And a robin sings
   In the holly-bush.

Full of fresh scents
   Are the budding boughs
Arching high over
   A cool green house;

Full of sweet scents,
   And whispering air
Which sayeth softly:
   'We spread no snare;

'Here dwell in safety,
   Here dwell alone,
With a clear stream
   And a mossy stone.

'Here the sun shineth
   Most shadily;
Here is heard an echo
   Of the far sea,
   Though far off it be.'
      Christina Rossetti [1830–1894]

Wild Roses

On long, serene midsummer days
  Of ripening fruit and yellow grain,
How sweetly, by dim woodland ways,
  In tangled hedge or leafy lane,
Fair wild-rose thickets, you unfold
Those pale pink stars with hearts of gold!

Your sleek patrician sisters dwell
  On lawns where gleams the shrub's trim bosk,
In terraced gardens, tended well,
  Near pebbled walk and quaint kiosk.
In costliest urns their colors rest;
They beam on beauty's fragrant breast!

But you in lowly calm abide,
  Scarce heeded save by breeze or bee;
You know what splendor, pomp and pride
  Full oft your brilliant sisters see;
What sorrow too, and bitter fears;
What made farewells and hopeless tears.

How some are kept in old, dear books,
  That once in bridal wreaths were worn;
How some are kissed, with tender looks,
  And later tossed aside with scorn;
How some their taintless petals lay
On icy foreheads, pale as they!

So, while these truths you vaguely guess,
  A-bloom in many a lonesome spot,
Shy roadside roses, may you bless
  The fate that rules your modest lot,
Like rustic maids that meekly stand
Below the ladies of their land!

Edgar Fawcett [1847–1904]

116

Acknowledgements

I would like to thank the following individuals who have allowed me to roam freely in their gardens and select the best specimens to photograph: John Tomlinson of Butchart Gardens; Susan Moody of The Cloisters; Karen Dardick of Descanso Gardens; Sandy Scott and Lucy Tolmach of Filoli; James P. Folsom and John Trager of Huntington Botanical Gardens; Colvin Randall and Sharon Fisher of Longwood Gardens; Carl A. Totemeier, Jr. and Leonard Marino of New York Botanical Gardens; Nancy Gorkin and Kim Johnson of Old Westbury Gardens.

In Brooklyn Botanic Garden, special thanks are due to rosarian Stephen Scanniello, who was kind enough to review the text for this book and Peter Malins, retired rosarian, who shared his knowledge and for many years inspired my photography with his love of roses.

I would also like to thank Lily Poskus for her inspiration and Solveig Williams for her creative insight in helping to realize a dream—"The Romantic Rose."

The poem *June* on page 100 and the quotations by Vita Sackville-West in the introductory text are reprinted with permission of Atheneum Publishers, and imprint of Macmillan Publishing Company, from Vita Sackville-West: *Illustrated Garden Book*, copyright © 1986 by Nigel Nicolson.